WILLS FOR WASHINGTON

WILLS FOR WASHINGTON
How to make your own will

Fred Hopkins, J.D.

Self-Counsel Press Inc.
a subsidiary of
International Self-Counsel Press Ltd.
U.S.A. Canada

Printed in Canada

First edition: July, 1977
Second edition: March, 1980
Third edition: July, 1982
Fourth edition: May, 1985
Fifth edition: May, 1992
Sixth edition: March, 1996

Cataloguing in Publication Data
Hopkins, Fred, 1952-
Wills for Washington

(Self-counsel legal series)
First - 5th eds. written by D. Van Fredenberg.
ISBN 1-55180-021-7

1. Wills — Washington (State) — Popular works. 2. Probate law and practice — Washington (State) — Popular works.
I. Van Fredenberg, D., 1911- Wills for Washington. II. Title.
III. Series.
KFW144.Z9V36 1995 346.79705'4 C95-910747-9

Self-Counsel Press Inc.
1704 N. State Street
Bellingham, Washington 98225
a subsidiary of
International Self-Counsel Press Ltd.
1481 Charlotte Road
North Vancouver, British Columbia
Canada V7J 1H1

With genuine acknowledgment to Chris Hancock, Esquire, for his invaluable assistance.

To Lisa, Lizabeth, and Dominic.

CONTENTS

SAMPLES

DISCLAIMER

Laws are constantly changing. The author, the publisher, and the vendor make no representation or warranties regarding the outcome or the use to which the information in this book is put and are not assuming any liability for any claims, losses, or damages arising out of the use of this book. The reader should not rely on the author or publisher of this book for any professional advice. Please be sure that you have the most recent edition. If you have any doubts whatsoever, consult an attorney.

1

ALL ABOUT WILLS

a. WHAT IS A WILL?

You've probably seen countless movies and plays involving eager heirs anxiously attending a reading of the will. You probably have a pretty accurate idea of what a will physically looks like, along with a dated picture of a stodgy old lawyer solemnly reading its provisions.

There may be some truth to these old representations, but the system is less formal now. One thing remains the same — the fundamental human need to direct how one's property is distributed after one's death. The ancient adage that "you can't take it with you" still holds true. After all, you don't see many moving vans following hearses.

People have always had a strong desire to control the disposition of their estates after death. The right to make wills existed in ancient Egypt, Assyria, and Babylon, as well as among the Hebrews, Greeks, and ancient Romans. The foundation and origin of English and American law concerning wills began in the mid-sixteenth century with the enactment of the "Statute of Wills" which authorized men to pass "real" property with a written will. A later English statute made a similar provision for "personal" property. (By real property we mean real estate; that is, land and any structures built on the land. By personal property we mean any type of property other than real estate and the additions to real estate.)

Wills, like any other legal document, have to be done right. No other document, if done improperly or carelessly, is more likely to end up in the courts or more subject to bitter family-splitting litigation.

A will becomes effective upon your death. It directs how your worldly possessions are to be divided among the persons named in that will. It tells your personal representative how your possessions are to be distributed.

Generally, a will authorizes someone you appoint to collect assets, pay off debts, and divide the property according to your wishes as set out in the will.

If you make a will, you are called a "testator," if a man or a "testatrix," if a woman. However, for ease of reading we shall use the form testator to apply to both men and women.

You might suppose that everyone has a "natural right" to dispose of whatever property he or she has collected during his or her lifetime. Not so. The right to make a will and to have it recognized by the courts is entirely statutory and can be tightly restricted and controlled by whatever government is in control in a particular jurisdiction.

The object of a will is to enable you, as the owner of property, to control its disposition at your death. The chief purpose of legislation on the subject is to ensure that your desires and intentions can be determined by those who will later read the document and put it into effect.

The various terms used, such as will, testament, last will, and last will and testament all mean the same thing. In fact, the title is the least important part of the document.

A will must have "testamentary character," that is, it must clearly show the intentions of the maker and confer no rights prior to death. It has no binding effect during your life, and you may revoke it whenever you wish. A will is intended to take effect only on your death.

b. WHO MAY MAKE A WILL?

In times past, and in different countries, various rules have prevailed. Some countries declared that no one could control his or her property after death and that all property passed on to the state.

Some laws provided that only men could make wills. Others limited the privilege to "free" men. But in the United States including, of course, the state of Washington, it has long been the rule that anyone of sound mind and legal age (18 years in Washington state) could leave a will that would control the disposition of his or her estate upon death.

It should, of course, be understood that when we talk about the disposition of your estate, we mean the net estate after the payment of any bills you may leave behind and any state or federal taxes which may be assessed.

A member of the armed forces of the United States or a person employed in the U.S. Merchant Marine may make what is known as a "nuncupative" will (oral will). The will may dispose of wages or personal property only. Only members of the armed forces of the United States or persons employed in the U.S. Merchant Marine may make nuncupative wills in Washington.

Such an oral will may be proved by two witnesses who were present and can testify that the testator spoke the words describing who was to have the estate. Any such proof must be offered in court within six months after those words were uttered, and the words must be put in writing and a citation (notice) issued to the surviving spouse or statutory heirs at law, so that they may, if desired, contest such a will. This type of will is not favored in the law because of the great opportunity for fraud.

This book is only about wills prepared and signed within the state of Washington. However, if a person dies here leaving a will that is not precisely in accord with the statutes of Washington, but was executed outside the state of Washington in the manner prescribed by the law of the testator's domicile or the place where the will was executed, it shall be deemed to be legally executed and may be admitted to probate in this state. However, it may be subject to Washington state laws involving community property and many other issues.

c. WHY SHOULD YOU MAKE A WILL?

Most people work hard during their lifetime to accumulate their assets and, by means of a will, they are able to provide after their death for their loved ones, donate to their favorite charities or causes, or help perpetuate whatever was of most importance to them while they were alive. Whatever you want to do with your estate, it should comfort you to know that, if you make a will, your wishes for the most part will be carried out.

But even if you take the attitude that it really doesn't matter after you have gone, consider the importance of a will as it might affect the lives of those you leave behind. A will not only greatly simplifies the distribution of an estate, but it also directs to whom it shall go and, perhaps, how it shall be used. It is usually enough of a shock for someone to lose a spouse, a family member, or a close friend without being left with the unnecessary burden and uncertainties of disposing of the deceased's estate.

Without provisions in a will, such as a trust, many children would not receive the education they deserve. Charities receive a substantial amount of their revenues from the estates of thoughtful people. Most of us have been the recipients of unrewarded kindnesses, and a provision in a will may be an excellent way of rewarding someone.

Of course, if you have a yen to be remembered, there is no better way than by leaving a specific gift or a specific amount of money to be used in a particular manner. Many churches and educational institutions (private and public) have programs to enable people to make a provision providing for them in their wills. For relatively modest estates, however, the primary people to be taken care of are, of course, your surviving spouse and children, and by making a will you can ease their transition to living without you.

d. WHAT HAPPENS IF YOU DIE WITHOUT A WILL?

If you die without a will, an exhaustive search of all of your belongings will be carried out and inquiries made of your banks, friends, and others in an effort to locate a will. Your spouse or eldest child or anyone interested in the will just won't be able to understand why such a thoughtful person as yourself just didn't get around to making one.

1. Who will be the personal representative?

However, if you do die "intestate," that is, without leaving a legal will, your spouse, a next-of-kin, a friend, or a creditor may apply to have the courts appoint the applicant or some other suitable person as the "administrator"* of the estate. If the estate is at all complicated, an individual, even a friend, may not want to take on the job, in which case the court would appoint a stranger to administer the estate. If the estate is substantial, a corporate personal representative, usually a national bank or trust company, may be appointed.

Needless to say, such a procedure is much more time-consuming, complicated, and probably more costly than appointing someone in your will. In addition, except in cases where a bank or a surviving spouse is appointed and the entire estate goes to the spouse or children, the administrator appointed must purchase and post a corporate bond from a bonding company to ensure faithful performance of the duties of administrator. (Bonding companies are listed in the yellow pages of the telephone book under "Bonds — surety and fidelity.")

---

* **Note:** The female form is "administratrix," but for ease of reading we will use only "administrator."

A will-appointed personal representative, generally called an "executor" ("executrix"),** may be appointed the same day the will is filed and may be granted wide discretionary powers. In fact, the laws of the state of Washington empower a personal representative named in a will to handle the estate without further intervention of the court, when your will so provides.

2. Who will receive your property?

If you die intestate (without a will) leaving no surviving spouse, children, or other relatives who can be located, then the entire estate is said to "escheat" and passes to the state of Washington. So, if you do not have any relatives, it is still advisable for you to make a will. If you would rather have your estate go to a favorite charity, to a friend, neighbor, or any person or cause of your choice, you must leave a valid will.

Most people, however, do leave behind relatives of some kind and if they do not have a will, their estates will be distributed among these relatives in accordance with the Washington state laws of "descent and distribution."

Here is how your estate will be distributed if you do not leave a will.

If all of the property of you and your spouse is community property and you leave no will, everything will go to your surviving spouse, to the exclusion of children or other heirs.

This is so, of course, only on the first death in a marriage. After the first spouse dies, all of the estate of the survivor is separate property.

Next, say that you are not married or that some or all of your property is separate property (i.e., belongs to you

---

** **Note**: The term "executor" may be used to refer to male or female, but, technically, a named female is an "executrix." However, if you don't like either term, use "personal representative."

alone). Washington law on descent and distribution provides that your separate property would be disposed of by the probate court as follows:

(a) One-half to spouse and one-half to children

(b) If no children, three-fourths to spouse and one-fourth to parents

(c) If no children or parents, three-fourths to spouse, one-fourth to brothers and sisters

(d) If no spouse, all to children

(e) If no spouse or children, all to parents

(f) If no spouse, children, or parents, all to brothers and sisters

(g) If no spouse, children, parents, or brothers and sisters, all to grandparents

(h) If no spouse, children, parents, brothers and sisters, or grandparents, all to children of grandparents

(i) If no issue (children or their children), parents, brothers and sisters, all to spouse

The statute on descent and distribution is referred to only to the extent that a will does not leave the estate to specific persons or organizations.

3. Minor children

If minor children may be left after your death, one very important use of the will is to name a guardian for these children in case the other parent is not living at the time of your death, or you are both involved in a fatal accident. It is true that the nomination of a guardian in your will is not binding on the courts, but it is given great weight and will be honored unless good reason is shown why someone else should be appointed.

e. ANOTHER REASON FOR A WILL — TAXES!

Not too many people need to be concerned about taxes after they die. Until January 1, 1982, Washington state had an inheritance tax law which generated about $53,000,000 per year for the government. Now, however, that tax has been removed from the law.

It has been replaced by a Washington state Estate Tax, which is a portion allowable under the Internal Revenue Code. If any tax is due under this federal law, then a tax shall be due to the state of Washington equal to the maximum amount of credit allowable under the Internal Revenue Code. The federal tax allows a "credit" to be deducted from the estate tax in an amount indicated by a table provided for that purpose.

This procedure is rather complicated, and these calculations are not for the amateur. Here is just one example of this "pickup" tax.

Suppose that, after exclusions and the unified credit, an estate remains that is taxable to $140,000 under the Internal Revenue Code. The credit for the state death taxes would be $1,200, which would be paid to the state of Washington. This $1,200 does not add to the total tax, but is a form of revenue-sharing by the federal government.

Other than this pickup tax, the only tax on estates in the state of Washington is the federal estate and gift tax. Both taxes use the same tables, percentages, and exclusions to calculate exemptions and it is possible to use up all exemptions to the estate tax during your lifetime. However, to do so you would have to have much more money than is in the average estate.

Gifts up to $10,000 per person per year may be made without any tax consequence at all, and an individual may give $10,000 each year to as many people or organizations as desired. A husband and wife may double that amount. For gifts larger than that, a tax return must be filed. In addition, a person may make gifts, either during his or her lifetime or in his or her will, totalling $600,000 tax-free. This amount is doubled in the case of a husband and wife.

Gifts and estates passing between husband and wife may now be in unlimited amounts. This is known as the unlimited marital deduction. The unlimited marital deduction does not apply to non-citizen spouses. If you are in this situation, you should consult an attorney.

Another recent liberal provision was the abolition of the "three-year exclusion rule." Formerly, gifts made within three years of death were presumed to have been made "in contemplation of death" and so were included in the donor's estate. Now, any gift within the above limits, made at any time, is tax-free.

If you feel that desired gifts or your estate will exceed $600,000 (including all life insurance policies), by all means, talk to your lawyer about estate planning. Of course, estate planning is always wise if you don't want to worry about estate taxes.

In estimating the value of your estate, keep in mind that Washington is a community property state. The terms "community property" and "separate property" may be unfamiliar to you. There are only nine community property states in the U.S. They are Washington, Idaho, Arizona, Nevada, New Mexico, California, Texas, Louisiana, and Wisconsin. There are some variations between these states, but in the state of Washington all property owned prior to marriage or acquired later by gift or inheritance, and in each case kept separate, is separate property. This includes the profits from such property as long as no post-marital effort or labor is spent collecting said profits. All other property acquired by husband and wife is community property. This means that only one-half of the community property is in the estate of each spouse. But after the first spouse dies, whatever property is left to the survivor will become part of the survivor's estate, thereby increasing the size of the survivor's estate.

The rules pertaining to community and separate ownership are quite complex. If it is important to you to clearly distinguish separate and community property, you should seek professional advice.

The status of your property could be very important if you are about to embark on a second marriage. You and your new spouse may have unequal amounts of property, or perhaps there are children by your first marriage you wish to protect. In this circumstance, it might be wise to consider a pre-marital agreement to avoid marital discord.*

f. DO YOU NEED A LAWYER?

There are certain categories of people who should always seek legal counsel before drawing up a will.

1. People about to be married

The will that you have now will be invalid for your new spouse. Don't delay in making a new will until you return from your honeymoon. Unfortunately, there have been many tragic accidents during honeymoons, and subsequent legal complications. If this is your second marriage and there are children on one or both sides; if say, you have more property than your spouse; or, if there is a marked difference in your ages, you would be wise to seek professional advice.

In any case, making a new will should be your first order of business. For use in a comparatively uncomplicated situation, see the samples in chapter 2.

In addition to making a new will, many people find it advisable to enter into a pre-marital agreement. Such an agreement should list the assets each party is bringing into

Note: Pre-marital or pre-nuptial agreements are not always enforced by Washington courts.

the new marriage and state which, if any, of those assets are to be kept as separate property and which are to be considered community property of the new marital community.

Maybe you want to keep separate from the new community a certain insurance policy, a bank account, certain corporate stock, or certain personal property, such as china or silverware. This agreement is usually considered especially important if there are children, particularly minor children, on one or both sides.

2. Owners of large or complex estates

People in this category should definitely consult their lawyers for tax planning. Thousands of dollars can be saved through adequate planning and tax avoidance. Foreign property interests, business arrangements, provision for cash for taxes and estate settlement — these and other technical matters usually call for legal counsel.

3. People about to be or recently divorced

Often people who are in the midst of a long divorce are counseled to make divorce wills, whereby the testator specifically states that his or her spouse is not to receive anything beyond his or her community property interest and that the remainder of the testator's estate is to go to other named parties. You should not consider the divorce process complete until you have signed a new will. The lawyer who handled your divorce might be the best person to consult.

4. Elderly people

See chapter 2, section **b.** for further information.

5. People making bequests to minors

If you intend to make a substantial bequest to a minor, you must appoint a guardian or establish a trust to handle the money or other property. You would be wise to consult a lawyer.

Another device for leaving a gift to a minor is the Uniform Transfers to Minors Act. Under this act, gifts may be made to minors during your lifetime, or incorporated in your will to take effect when your estate is distributed.

The custodian of the money or other property occupies much the same position as a trustee; it is to the custodian that the property is left. That custodian may be any adult person or a financial institution that is insured as provided by the statute or, in some cases, a trust company.

Each gift may be made to only one minor, and only one person may be the custodian. The custodian may decide how much money may be spent for the care of a minor beneficiary with or without regard to the ability of the minor to support himself or herself or the obligation of any other person to support the said minor.

When the minor reaches the age of 14 years, a parent or guardian may petition the court for an order requiring the custodian to pay to the minor as much of the custodial property as is necessary for the minor's support, maintenance, or education. The statute provides no standards for such decisions.

Any unexpended funds must be turned over to the beneficiary when he or she turns 21 years old.

Because the custodian has some control over how the money is expended, and because this is an irrevocable transaction, you may want to talk to your lawyer before leaving a gift of this kind.

Will-making is like medical care — you may be able to take care of an ordinary scratch, cut, or bruise, but if you are not sure, see your doctor.

g. HOW MUCH WILL A LAWYER CHARGE?

The best way to find out how much a lawyer will charge is to ask. After a few minutes in conference with a lawyer, during which you may relate the extent of your estate and your basic desires concerning its disposition, a lawyer will be able to quote you a fee.

In more complex estates, there may be an hourly charge, which will be quoted on request. In any event, the peace of mind that accompanies the knowledge that the document is properly drawn and executed, and that you are advised of all appropriate options, is an important consideration that is hard to reduce to a monetary value. When you evaluate the fee charged by a lawyer, consider the value to your family or other heirs of receiving a well-planned and unassailable estate disposition plan.

It is always advisable to consult an attorney if at all possible.

2

DRAFTING YOUR OWN WILL

a. THE REQUIREMENTS OF A VALID WILL

1. Legal requirements

(a) You must be of legal age — in the state of Washington, that is 18 years old.

(b) The will must be in writing. This means it must be handwritten, printed, typed, or by any other means put in readable form so that it can be admitted in court as evidence of your intentions. A will does not have to be written in any set form, but you are advised to follow what is known as a "precedent," that is, a guide or example that has been used successfully before. (See Samples #1 and #2).

(c) The will must be signed by you (the testator or testatrix) or some other person at your direction and in your presence. Ideally, of course, you would sign your name exactly as it appears on the written will. If the name by which you are generally known is markedly different from your true name, that fact should be set forth on the signature page.

If you are physically unable to sign your name, you may affix your "mark" to the document. This is usually an X, but any mark will do as long as it can be testified to by the witnesses to the will that you intended to and did make the mark as your signature to your will.

SAMPLE #1
GENERAL FORM OF A WILL

LAST WILL AND TESTAMENT

I, Tom Turf, of King County, Washington, being of sound and disposing mind and memory, and not acting under duress, menace, fraud, or undue influence, do hereby make, publish, and declare this my LAST WILL AND TESTAMENT.

I.

I hereby declare that I am not married nor have I ever been married, and I have no children.

II.

I hereby give and bequeath unto Benny Track the sum of $500 dollars.

III.

I hereby give, devise, and bequeath unto my sister, Tara Turf, all the rest, residue, and remainder of my estate, whether real or personal, and wheresoever located; provided, however, in the event that Tara Turf shall predecease me, or die within 30 days after my death, then and in that event, I give, devise, and bequeath unto my only nephew, Thomas Turf, all the rest, residue, and remainder of my estate, whether real or personal, and wheresoever located.

IV.

I hereby nominate and appoint Tara Turf as Executrix of this, my Last Will and Testament, to act without bond. In the event that Tara Turf is for any reason unable or unwilling to act as Executrix hereof, or fails to complete the administration of my estate, I nominate and appoint Thomas Turf to act as Executor hereof, also without bond.

V.*

I hereby direct that my estate be settled without intervention of any court, except to the extent required by law, and that my Executrix settle my estate in such manner as shall seem best and most convenient to her (him), and I hereby empower my Executrix to mortgage, lease, sell, exchange, and convey the personal and real property of my estate without an order of court for that purpose and without notice, approval, or

*The "non-intervention" clause in paragraph V allows the personal representative to handle the probate without going to the probate court to secure permission or approval of the payment of bills or distribution of the estate, and in general to supervise the handling of the probate. If you think that some heirs might be difficult, or that the executor might not relish the responsibility, then you may want to omit that clause. However, the giving of non-intervention powers expedites the probate process and removes much of the complaint about the amount of time required to settle an estate.

SAMPLE #1 — Continued

confirmation, and in all other respects to administer and settle my estate without the intervention of court.

VI.

I hereby revoke any and all former Wills and Codicils made by me and declare this my Last Will and Testament.

IN WITNESS WHEREOF, I have hereunto set my hand this 20th day of January, 199 —.

Tom Turf
____
(*Testator*)

STATE OF WASHINGTON

COUNTY OF KING

Ima G. Witness and Ura G. Witness being first duly sworn, on oath depose and say:

That this affidavit is made by the attesting witnesses to the Last Will and Testament of Tom Turf, who executed the foregoing instrument, consisting of two pages, on January 20, 199 —, in the presence of each of us, and who did thereupon publish and declare the same to be his (her) Last Will and Testament, and we, the undersigned, at his (her) request and in his (her) presence, and in the presence of each other, hereunto subscribed our names as witnesses thereto. That said Testator, at the time of executing said Will, was over the age of 18 years and appeared to be of sound mind and acting freely and voluntarily, without any duress or undue influence whatsoever. That we are competent and over the age of 18 years.

Ima G. Witness residing at Seattle, Washington

Ura G. Witness residing at Seattle, Washington

SUBSCRIBED AND SWORN to before me this 20th day of January, 199 —.

Nathan Notary
____
NOTARY PUBLIC in and for
the State of Washington,
residing at Seattle.

The foregoing instrument, consisting of two typewritten pages, of which this is the last, was on the date thereof signed and published by Tom Turf, who, at said time, appeared to be of sound and disposing mind and memory, and was by him declared to be his Last Will and Testament, in the presence of us, who, at his request and in his presence and in the presence of each other, have hereunto set out hands as witnesses thereto this 20th day of January, 199 —. Each page of this Will bears the signature of the Testator.

Ima G. Witness residing at Seattle, Washington

Ura G. Witness residing at Seattle, Washington

If you are absolutely unable to sign your name or even to make your mark, then the signature may be signed by some other person who would do so at your direction and in your presence. If this situation occurs, the person should sign your name, then state that he or she has subscribed your name at your request, and finally sign his or her own name.

(d) The will must be "attested" to by two or more competent witnesses who must sign their names to the will in your presence and at your direction or request. To be legally "competent" the witness must be over age 18.

All wills, including a holographic will (one completely in the testator's own handwriting) must be properly witnessed to be a valid will for Washington residents.

SAMPLE #2
ALTERNATIVE FORM OF A WILL

LAST WILL AND TESTAMENT

I, Barney Brown, of King County, Washington, being of sound and disposing mind and memory and not acting under duress, menace, fraud, or undue influence, do hereby make, publish, and declare this my Last Will and Testament.

I.

I declare that Bette Brown is my wife and so referred to herein; that we have three children now living, namely, Beverly Brown, Beth Brown, and Bobby Brown. At the date of this instrument, there are no lineal descendants of deceased children (i.e., grandchildren or great-grandchildren.)

II.

To my said children, including any who may later be born to or adopted by us, I leave no estate, knowing that my wife will properly care for them.

III.

To my wife I give, devise, and bequeath all of my property, of every kind, nature, or description, real, personal, or mixed, separate and community, wheresoever situated and howsoever and whensoever acquired, owned by me, or to which I may be entitled at the time of my death.

IV.

In the event that my wife shall predecease me, or die within thirty (30) days after my death, then and in that event I give, devise, and bequeath my entire estate unto my children, share and share alike.

V.

I hereby nominate and appoint Bette Brown as the Executrix of this, my Last Will and Testament, to act without bond. In the event that Bette Brown is for any reason unable or unwilling to act as such, or fails to

BB initials Apr 30, 9- date

complete the administration of my estate, I nominate and appoint Billie Blue to act as Executor hereof, also without bond.

VI.

I hereby direct that my estate be settled without intervention of any court, except to the extent required by law, and that my Executrix settle my estate in such manner as shall seem best and most convenient to her (him), and I hereby empower my Executrix to mortgage, lease, sell, exchange and convey the personal and real property of my estate without an order of court for that purpose and without notice, approval, or confirmation, and in all other respects to administer and settle my estate without the intervention of court.

VII.

I hereby revoke all former Wills and codicils made by me.

IN WITNESS WHEREOF, I have hereunto set my hand this 30th day of April, 199 —.

Barney Brown
(Testator)

STATE OF WASHINGTON

COUNTY OF KING

Ima G. Witness and Ura G. Witness being first duly sworn, on oath depose and say:

That this affidavit is made by the attesting witnesses to the Last Will and Testament of Barney Brown, who executed the foregoing instrument, consisting of two pages, on April 30, 199 —, in the presence of each of us, and who did thereupon publish and declare the same to be his (her) Last Will and Testament, and we, the undersigned, at his (her) request and in his (her) presence, and in the presence of each other, hereunto subscribed our names as witnesses thereto. That said Testator, at the time of executing said Will, was over the age of 18 years and appeared to be of sound mind

BB initials Apr 30, 9- date

SAMPLE #2 — Continued

and acting freely and voluntarily, without any duress or undue influence whatsoever. That we are competent and over the age of 18 years.

Ima G. Witness residing at Seattle, Washington

Ura G. Witness residing at Seattle, Washington

SUBSCRIBED AND SWORN to before me this 30th day of April, 199 —.

Nathan Notary
NOTARY PUBLIC in and for
the State of Washington,
residing at Seattle.

The foregoing instrument, consisting of two typewritten pages, of which this is the last, was on the date thereof signed, initialed, and published by Barney Brown, who, at said time, appeared to be of sound and disposing mind and memory, and was by him declared to be his Last Will and Testament, in the presence of us, who, at his request and in his presence and in the presence of each other, have hereunto set our hands as witnesses thereto this 30th day of April, 199 —. Each page of this will bears the signature of the testator.

Ima G. Witness residing at Seattle, Washington

Ura G. Witness residing at Seattle, Washington

BB initials *Apr 30, 9*–date

Though only two competent and disinterested witnesses are necessary, it does no harm to have more than two sign as witnesses. The affidavit now commonly used at the end of the will that has been adopted in this state is shown in Sample #1 and Sample #2.

The affidavit is now authorized in place of the written testimony of the witnesses to be filed when the will is offered for probate. However, the wording is such that it doubles as an attestation clause and testimony. Before the adoption of this form, it was necessary to locate the witnesses and either bring them into court to testify or to have them sign out-of-court affidavits to the effect that they were, in fact, the witnesses who signed the will at the direction of the testator, and that they observed that the person making the will was of sound mind. Now, however, with the new form, it is not necessary to bring the witnesses into court or to secure their signature to any other document.

(**Warning:** *Do not* have a beneficiary under the will sign as a witness. In general, if a named beneficiary signs as a witness, a gift in the will is invalid as to that witness. There are other ramifications to the statute which announces this rule, but take no chances — use witnesses who are not beneficiaries.)

2. Recommended procedure

You will note that most attestation clauses to wills include the phrase that the person making the will "...published and declared the same to be his (or her) last will and testament..." While it is not legally necessary for you to declare this, it is considered good policy to do so. Such a statement advises the witnesses directly that you know what you are signing and it expresses your intentions in the matter. In other words, the clause is just one little precaution that could save later arguments or possible lawsuits.

Note also that the only statutory requirement of anyone signing in the presence of anyone else is of the witnesses signing in the presence of the person making the will. However, again, it is considered the best practice, and another means of avoiding later discussions about the facts surrounding the signing of the will, for you, the testator, and the two witnesses (and, if one is used, a notary public) to be together for the signing of the will. You must sign first, then, at your direction and request, the two witnesses sign in your presence and in the presence of each other. The notary public should sign last.

b. TESTAMENTARY CAPACITY

Occasionally a will may be contested in court by disgruntled heirs who allege that the person making the will was subject to "undue influence" in the naming of his or her principal beneficiaries. Most of these suits in effect challenge the "testamentary capacity" of the person making the will, alleging that he or she was ill, old, enfeebled, or otherwise generally incapable of arriving at an independent decision about the disposition of his or her estate and perhaps unaware of the extent of the estate or the recipients of the gifts.

However, if the will has been drawn up in a legally acceptable way and is rational on its face, testamentary capacity is presumed, and it is presumed that the will speaks the wishes of the person making it. It is said that a person contesting a will has the burden of proving lack of capacity by "clear, cogent, and convincing" evidence. This is one of the most difficult obligations to fulfill in the trial of any lawsuit.

Various cases have announced decisions to the general effect that age, disease, disposition, temper, eccentricity, stinginess, spendthriftiness, or other "peculiarities" are not enough to bar the admission of a legal last will and testament.

While a will contest does on occasion succeed, it is obvious that there is a strong presumption in favor of validity. The essence of a valid will is that you, the testator, knew and understood the extent and nature of your estate and the recipients of your gifts. You do not have to understand all of the possible legal ramifications of the document. You do, however, have to know and understand the contents of the will, the extent and nature of your estate, and to whom your estate will be given upon your death.

If there is a substantial question concerning the capacity of a person to make a will, a lawyer should be employed to prepare the document. In this way, a professional opinion will be available in case of a challenge of capacity when the will is offered for probate. Incidentally, this is another reason for having a notary public sign your will.

c. TO WHOM MUST YOU LEAVE SOMETHING?

To no one, that's to whom.

Keep in mind that in the state of Washington all property acquired after marriage, except by gift or inheritance or pursuant to contractual agreement, is generally community property. As such, one-half belongs to each of the marriage partners. Hence, husband and wife each have the right to dispose in their wills of only one-half of the community property. For instance, if the wife dies, her surviving husband automatically retains one-half of the community property, but does not automatically receive his wife's half — she may have left a will giving her half of the property to someone else.

While no one must be left anything, it is, however, necessary and vital that you include in your will a paragraph naming your wife or husband and all of your children, natural and adopted, by this marriage or otherwise. If you do not, then regardless of the terms of the will, these omitted heirs will inherit from you what they would have received had there been no will. Their entitlement in this case would be in accordance with the statute of descent and distribution (see chapter 1, section **d.**). If, for example, in your will you fail to mention your wife, she would inherit all of your portion of the community property and one-half of your separate property, if any, even though your will has left your entire estate to other people. This is what the term "pretermitted heirs" means.

The rationale is that the spouse and children are usually the most natural objects of a deceased's bounty, and failure to mention them might indicate that you lack testamentary capacity or that you forgot such close relatives. They must be mentioned.

If, however, any heir other than a surviving spouse or child predeceases you, a bequest to such a person "lapses" and goes into the residue of your estate. If you want to ensure against that possibility, name an alternative beneficiary, either a person or an organization.

Incidentally, this may be a good place to point out the durable quality of a will. A will is unique in that the failure of one part does not necessarily invalidate the balance of it. If only one portion of a will is valid, it is entitled to be admitted to probate, even though other parts may be invalidated because of fraud, undue influence, or mistake. The all-important factor is the general intent of the person who made the will.

d. HOW IS A WILL REVOKED?

A will is revoked by its destruction by, or at the direction of, its maker, or by the making of a new will.

If a second will is drawn and intended to supersede the first will, then the first one should be destroyed. The best way of ensuring that your will has been revoked is to destroy it.

If it is accidentally burned or otherwise destroyed, it is not revoked. But you should immediately make up a new one from a photocopy of your will if you made one.

Note: *Do not* keep a *signed* photocopy unless you keep track of the location of all signed copies. Signed photocopies are originals. There should only be one valid signed will in existence at any one time.

If you destroy or change your will you must retrieve and destroy all earlier signed photocopies. You do not want to create confusion by having two signed but different wills in existence.

On rare occasions it is possible to prove the existence of a lost will, and there are special laws about the procedure. If the instructions contained in the lost will can be proven, the deceased's assets will pass in accordance with them.

A will may also be revoked by operation of law. We have noted that a partial revocation occurs if you marry or fail to mention a spouse or child in your will. The same partial revocation occurs if you obtain a divorce. That is, the will is automatically revoked concerning your divorced spouse. Obviously, upon the entry of a divorce decree you immediately need a new will.

Incidentally, a will, once revoked, is a nullity and is not revived by revoking a later will. If the terms of the first will are desired, a new will must be prepared and signed, or a codicil must be prepared to amend the second will (see Sample #6).

e. SPECIAL CLAUSES

A variety of special clauses may be used in your will to further specify your wishes. In addition to those discussed below, see the clauses in the Appendix.

1. Domicile

It is advisable to include a "domicile" clause indicating in what legal jurisdiction you signed the will and where you consider your domicile or residence to be.

If you are one of those who, being retired and on a comfortable pension, are spending about half of each year in warmer climes, and perhaps have financial interests in another state, you may want to consult a lawyer about tax planning for your estate. There are sometimes lengthy and expensive arguments about which state has a right to tax "transitory," or personal, property. There are different rules about the location of real and of personal property for tax purposes.

If you have enough involvements or wealth to really worry about taxes, see a lawyer.

2. Revocation

While the signing of a will automatically revokes any prior ones, it is considered another safety factor to include a clause saying: "I hereby revoke any and all previous wills and codicils by me heretofore made."

When the new will is signed, destroy the prior one.

3. Signing

While a will *must* be signed at the end by you, it is considered good practice for you to sign each page of the will, on the theory that this could prevent some unscrupulous person from substituting one of the pages of the will for one more agreeable to that person.

4. Naming executor

While is it not a legal requirement of a valid will, nevertheless one of the important reasons for having a will is to name a personal representative to act as the executor of the will. Such a person has the responsibility of gathering up and accounting for all of the assets of the estate and disposing of them properly.

Needless to say, such a person should understand the estate you will leave and have the time and inclination to perform the prescribed duties diligently. You may name as executor any adult person of sound mind who has not been convicted of a crime, or a bank that has a trust department.

In the small or average estates, it is usually satisfactory to name your spouse or adult son or daughter as executor. If these people are not suitable, perhaps another relative or close friend in whom you have confidence would be appropriate.

If a lawyer handles the probate of the estate, he or she will be able to advise your executor, so the one you name does not have to be experienced in these matters. However, for a substantial estate which may have settlement complications or tax problems, you may want to name a national bank, a lawyer, an accountant, or a knowledgeable business person, as personal representative or trustee.

Remember, if you have that kind of estate, the fee required by a lawyer to draft your will may be money well spent.

It could be that by the time the services of your named executor are needed, he or she is unable or unwilling to serve. If you have named a bank, the institution may decline because the estate is too small, or for other reasons. It is a good idea, therefore, to name an alternative executor, to serve only if the first one named does not serve or fails to complete the administration of the estate.

5. 30-day clause

Most will drafters include what is known as a "30-day clause" such as this:

> If my wife should survive me by 30 days, then I give, devise, and bequeath to her all of my property...

Such a clause doesn't mean much to you or to your spouse who might die within the 30 days as a result of, say, an accident in which both of you are killed at the same time or in which one lingers for a few days or weeks, but it can mean a great deal to the secondary heirs. It may affect the amount of tax owed.

When the first member of a married couple dies, one-half of the community property and all of the deceased's separate property is subject to tax. If all of it went to the surviving spouse, and that spouse were to die, say, two weeks later, then the first half of the property would be taxed again along with the half left by the second deceased spouse. The 30-day clause would cause the estate of the first descendent to pass directly to the secondary heirs and thus the estate would be taxed only once.

There is no requirement that such a clause must be 30 days; it could be shortened to 15 days, or extended to 60 days. However, since the purpose is to include some time period after which it is unlikely there would be a second death as the result of a common accident and still not unduly delay the administration of the estate, 30 days is the time period most commonly used.

If it is not known which member of the community died first, the Uniform Simultaneous Death Act specifies that the property of each spouse is distributed as though each had survived the other.

6. Alternative beneficiaries

The foregoing discussion should make it abundantly clear that it is highly advisable always to name alternative beneficiaries in your will. Sometimes, if there is even a remote chance that both the primary and secondary beneficiaries could die at or about the same time, it is considered advisable to name yet a third contigent beneficiary, for instance, your grandchildren.

7. Taxes

If your estate is large enough to be subject to estate taxes, you may put in a clause stating that all taxes shall be paid out of the "residue" of your estate (i.e., property not specifically bequeathed to anyone). Or, you may provide that the share of each recipient shall be charged with a proportionate part of the tax.

Usually payment from the residue is preferred. That way each heir knows how much will be received, and tax computation is much easier.

8. Personal effects

Particularly in the situation in which there are several beneficiaries including a surviving spouse, it is frequently deemed advisable to include a clause such as this:

> I give and bequeath all of my personal effects and all of our household furniture, furnishings, equipment, etc., to my wife.

This clause makes it unnecessary to account for the many small items in almost every estate and makes sure that they go to the person(s) who would make the best use of, and who would most care for, such things.

If you have a great number of items of personal property, such as a large assortment of valuable jewelry, silver, or *objets d'art,* you may, if you wish, list everything meticulously in your will, or you may find the following way more satisfactory. A Washington law allows you to dispose of "tangible personal property" by means of a separate written document, if you follow these steps. The document must be referred to in the Will; you can add a provision such as this in your Will:

> I instruct my Executor to follow instructions I may leave in a handwritten and signed document disposing of certain tangible personal property.

The document must describe the items of tangible personal property and the recipients with reasonable certainty. The document must be signed by the testator and should be handwritten.

What property can you leave this way? Items such as furniture, cars, jewelry, and art work are tangible personal property. The following items *cannot* be disposed of by this procedure: real estate, mobile homes, property used primarily in a trade or business, and intangible property such as currency, bank accounts, stocks, and bonds.

One of the big advantages of using this procedure is that you can change your mind any time you want without having to review your will or have a codicil written. All you have to do is write a new document (follow all the procedures described above) and throw away the old one. It's a good idea to date the document so that if two or more exist at the time of your death, your executor can tell which one was the most recent. Keep the original with your will.

9. Use of percentages

If you name several heirs to receive different shares, it is usually better to specify percentages of a fund or of the whole estate, rather than specific sums. Between the time of signing the will and your death, your estate may well be smaller, even dramatically so. If specific amounts of dollars are left, there just may not be enough to go around and accomplish whatever else you provided for in the will. A percentage, on the other hand, maintains the same ratio of division among the heirs.

10. Disposal of entire estate

If you do make a will that gives most of your estate to specified persons or organizations, always be sure to include a clause similar to the following, so that there will be no doubt that you have disposed of your entire estate:

> All of the rest, residue, and remainder of my property of whatsoever kind, nature, or description and wheresoever located, I give, devise, and bequeath to: (Here you may insert one or more names or organizations, or if the residue will be in some substance, you may dispose of it by percentages, as suggested above.)

11. Funeral arrangements

If you have any preferences about your funeral burial or cremation, you may express your desires in the will. Many people feel that the survivors should be consulted about this because they are the ones who will be most affected by whatever decision is made. Some people like to be more specific and to indicate such things as the maximum amount to be spent on a funeral, if any; the type of interment (if grave or a crypt); the disposition of the ashes (if cremation); the type of service — religious or lay, or one conducted by a fraternal organization.

12. Living Will

With the advance of medical care and the ability to prolong life, many people, particularly as they grow older, are concerned about becoming incurably ill, being maintained by artificial means so that all vital signs are intact, and being without any consciousness of themselves or those about them.

Washington law authorizes you to state your intentions in a document that is officially called a Directive to Physicians, but is also referred to as a Living Will. The language of the statute is shown in the example in Sample #3. The Living Will must be witnessed and attested to by two witnesses. It cannot be witnessed by the doctor or other health care professionals involved.

The Living Will only applies in limited situations, as you will see when you read the language. In recent years, many people have become concerned about being able to terminate medical treatment in other situations, for example, if death is not imminent, or if the medical treatment consists of food and water tubes. In the Directive to Physicians, you are required to initial whether or not you want artificially provided nutrition and hydration if you are in a terminal condition, or permanent unconscious condition. Recent Supreme Court decisions suggest that it is crucial, if you wish to have treatment terminated in situations such as that, that you state your intentions in writing. In addition to the required initialization, there are two recommended ways of doing this. First, you could add your own specific instructions to the Living Will. Second, you could prepare a "Medical Care Power of Attorney" which is now recognized by Washington law. In this document you can authorize a certain person to make medical care decisions for you if you are not competent to make them yourself, and you can add a paragraph stating any particular intentions or instructions you have.

13. Business interests

If you leave an active business when you die, one of the powers given to your executor should be:

> to continue the operation of any business in which I may have been engaged at the time of my death.

If this clause is not used, an administrator would have to secure a court order to continue your business during the period of probate.

f. SPECIFIC BEQUESTS

If you have certain relatives, friends, or organizations you wish to remember with a certain amount of money or certain items you feel they would like to have, you should include such directions in your will.

Strictly speaking, a "specific bequest" means either a certain object or money taken out of a certain described fund, such as:

> I leave to my uncle, Ralph Rover, out of my passbook savings account at the Old Reserve S & L Association, the sum of $_______ cash.

Such a bequest will be paid whether or not there is enough to cover all of the other bequests you have made. If you leave a specific sum out of your general estate to a certain person, that person will receive it in full if there are adequate funds in the estate but, if not, will receive a share in proportion to all of the other bequests.

It is usually best to leave heirlooms, antiques, and unique articles as specific bequests to people who you know will use them to the best advantage. Remember that not everyone would like that 120-year old rocker, and only an

SAMPLE #3
LIVING WILL

DIRECTIVE TO PHYSICIANS

I, ______________________________, having the capacity to make health care decisions, willfully and voluntarily make known my desire that my dying shall not be artificially prolonged under the circumstances set forth below, and do hereby declare that:

I

If at any time I should be diagnosed in writing to be in a terminal condition by the attending physician, or in a permanent unconscious condition by two physicians, and where the application of life-sustaining treatment would serve only to artificially prolong the process of my dying, I direct that such treatment be withheld or withdrawn, and that I be permitted to die naturally. I understand by using this form that a terminal condition means an incurable and irreversible condition caused by injury, disease, or illness, that would within reasonable medical judgment cause death within a reasonable period of time in accordance with accepted medical standards, and where the application of life-sustaining treatment would serve only to prolong the process of dying. I further understand in using this form that a permanent unconscious condition means an incurable and irreversible condition in which I am medically assessed within reasonable medical judgment as having no reasonable probability of recovery from an irreversible coma or a persistent vegetative state.

II

In the absence of my ability to give directions regarding the use of such life-sustaining treatment, it is my intention that this directive shall be honored by my family and physicians as the final expression of my legal right to refuse medical or surgical treatment, and I accept the consequences of such refusal. If another person is appointed to make these decisions for me, whether through a durable power of attorney or otherwise, I request that the person be guided by this directive and any other clear expressions of my desires.

III

If I am diagnosed to be in a terminal condition or in a permanent unconscious condition (initial one):

______ I <u>DO</u> want to have artificially provided nutrition and hydration.

______ I <u>DO NOT</u> want to have artificially provided nutrition and hydration.

SAMPLE #3 — Continued

IV

If I have been diagnosed as pregnant and that diagnosis is known to my physician, this directive shall have no force and effect during the course of my pregnancy.

V

I understand the full import of this directive, and I am emotionally and mentally competent to make this directive. I understand that before I sign this directive, I can add to or delete from or otherwise change the wording of this directive and that I may add to or delete from this directive at any time and that any changes shall be consistent with Washington state law or federal constitutional law to be legally valid.

VI

It is my wish that every part of this directive be fully implemented. If for any reason any part is held invalid it is my wish that the remainder of my directive be implemented.

Signed ______________________________

____
City, County, and State of Residence

Date ______________________________

I personally know the Declarer, and I believe him/her to be capable of making health care decisions.

____
WITNESS

____
WITNESS

informed person would appreciate the value of that old, uninspiring-looking basket.

If you are quite sure that there are going to be a lot of personal items left over, such as clothing, you might direct that they be given to a charity that would pass them on to someone who could well use them.

It is, of course, recommended that these types of specific bequests not be so numerous or so difficult to deliver that the chore in handling them in the estate far outweighs the appreciation with which they might be received. Remember that handling the estate of a deceased relative or friend is a task that no one really relishes, so you should make it as easy as possible.

Incidentally, you should always remember that your will has no effect until you die. Hence, even though you have designated a specific item of property in your will as going to say, Aunt Maude, you are not prohibited from selling or otherwise disposing of that item. If the object mentioned is no longer in your estate at the time of your death, then nothing happens except that the bequest fails and Aunt Maude will have to do without the treasure. In legal language, the legacy is "adeemed."

g. CHARITY

Your will is your last chance to give something to your favorite charity. There are many worthwhile organizations and causes, such as churches, children's groups, health organizations, and international welfare funds, most of which are in need of funds for the good work they carry on. If every person's will were to contain a modest percentage for charity, all of these organizations would probably have adequate funds. And remember, your bequest to a charity is, in practically all cases, tax-free. Just be sure to cite the correct name of the organization and the chapter you wish to benefit, such as: "National Association of Influenza, Seattle Chapter."

A relatively new clause that is found in numerous wills is one leaving your body, or parts of it, for humanitarian causes. In most metropolitan areas there are people awaiting a call from a doctor to be advised that there is a certain body part, such as an eye, available for transplanting. Such parts could well prolong the life of someone or make life considerably happier.

If you wish to include such a clause, one important thing to remember is that someone, preferably the executor of your estate, must receive word immediately upon your death so that the proper medical authorities may be notified. Any transplant must be made within a very short time after death. For the correct clause to be inserted in your will, it is recommended that you get in touch with the organization in your community that is involved with the part of the body you are considering leaving. They will advise you about the exact terminology to insert in your will and all the particulars about arrangements upon death.

If you wish to leave your whole body for research, you might direct that it go to the University of Washington Medical School.

You should also carry a card in your billfold or purse stating that, at your death, the appropriate medical foundation should be contacted immediately.

h. CAN YOU DISINHERIT A SPOUSE OR CHILD?

Many people believe that if they just leave $1 to a wife or child, they can successfully disinherit that wife or child. This is incorrect. In Washington, a surviving spouse may have set aside from the community property or the separate property of the deceased a "homestead" or, "in lieu of homestead," money or other property of the estate of the value of $30,000, valued as of the date of death.

Such an award is favored in law and is liberally construed by the courts. It protects surviving spouses and minor children and is to be applied regardless of whether it contradicts the deceased's wishes. The award is a matter of right to the surviving spouse, except, of course, to one who has feloniously killed his or her spouse.

The award is discretionary with the court if there are children of the deceased by a former marriage or adoption prior to the marriage to the petitioner, or if the petitioning surviving spouse has abandoned his or her minor children and has wrongfully failed to provide for them, or if the applicant or minor children are entitled to receive property or insurance in excess of $30,000 because of the death. In all of these cases the court shall decide what is fair under the circumstances.

If you do not mention your spouse or your children in your will, they will receive the share they would have received had you not left a will. And, of course, if you have read this far you know that all you are leaving is your separate property and your one-half of the community property.

If your intention is to disinherit your spouse and children, simply list them by name and say nothing further, or, preferably, say something like the following:

> I make no provision for them because they are otherwise cared for.
>
> My insurance will sufficiently provide for them.
>
> They have contributed nothing to my happiness.

For further information regarding the use or effect of homestead exemptions, consult an attorney. Also, further information will be found in *Probate Guide for Washington,* another title in the Self-Counsel Series.

i. SUPPOSE YOU MOVE TO ANOTHER STATE

Generally, if you move permanently to another state, your will will be valid if it is a legal will in the jurisdiction in which it was made. However, if you move and acquire property interests elsewhere, you should consult an attorney regarding tax problems, because you should have a new will made in your new domicile (home) state.

Washington's community property system is an example of different laws that only a few states have. Your move to another state is just one of the many circumstances which might demand that you make a new will.

j. SUPPOSE YOU OWN PROPERTY IN ANOTHER STATE

If you leave only "personal" property in another state, then it should all be included in the probate in Washington state.

If, however, you leave real property in another state, there would have to be what is known as an ancillary probate in that state. The reason for this is that personal property is said to be "ambulatory" and its ownership follows the domicile of its owner. Real estate, on the other hand, is an integral part of the state where it is located and is under the exclusive jurisdiction of that state. Then, too, the very manner in which title to real estate is recorded dictates that all of the records for it must be in the state where it's located.

Sometimes it is necessary if title or boundaries of a piece of real estate become confused, or for many other reasons, to trace title back to the original land grant from the government and the first survey. Such information is available only in the state in which the real estate is located.

Needless to say, even if you have only one piece of real estate in another state, the cost of probate would be proportionately larger than it would be for your principal and diversified estate in your own jurisdiction. You may feel that this would be a compelling reason to sell an isolated piece of property and to reinvest the money in your own state. Or, you may wish to investigate other means of controlling out-of-state property, such as through a corporation.

k. TRUSTS

1. General

Prior to January 1982, when the repeal of the state inheritance tax became effective, and prior to the dramatic increase in exemptions of federal estate laws, taxation provided one of the compelling reasons to have trusts. Now, however, there is no state tax reason and little federal tax reason for an individual estate of less than $600,000 to have trusts. Therefore, the principal reasons now for trusts for the average person are administrative considerations.

The law of trusts is a vast and complicated area of laws, rules, and regulations, many of which have intricate legal and tax complications. However, there are some simple ones which might be used to accomplish a specific purpose you may have in mind and possibly to save you some taxes.

Keep in mind that the tax savings, in most cases, do not occur upon the occasion of the first death, in the case of husband and wife, but only on the second. Trusts, of course, may be established in many forms and for various purposes, but this section concerns only testamentary trusts, i.e., trusts set up by a last will and testament.

Trusts may be set up for many useful purposes, but only some of the major uses will be discussed here. The terms of a trust regarding the expenditure of funds and how and when the trust will be placed in the control of the trustee may be extremely complicated. It is, however, good advice to "keep it simple" so that there will be no difficulty in understanding the trust's terms later and so that it will not be more of a burden than a help to those who must administer it and live under it.

2. For your children

If you are responsible for one or more minor children, two of your more important alternatives are as follows:

(a) You may leave all of your estate directly to the children, with the knowledge that the court will appoint a guardian to care for them personally and for their estate.

(b) You may, and should, name some relative or other suitable person to be the guardian. By doing so, you are in reality only nominating a person for that task, because your suggestion is not binding on the probate court. However, unless there are good reasons why your wishes should not be complied with, the Superior Court will almost always appoint the guardian whom you have named in the will.

If the person appointed is to be the guardian of both the persons and property of the minors, he or she will have complete control over the children, subject of course to court order. If, on the other hand, someone else has control of the persons of the minors, and your nominee is only the guardian of the estate of the children, then he or she will be concerned only with the funds which you have left for the care and support of the children.

In either case, the guardian is under court orders and can only make such expenditures as the court will allow. Annual reports to the court must be made and the guardian is under bond. The court looks after the interests of the children by seeing that they are cared for and that the assets of the estate are not wasted.

As an alternative to the guardianship proceedings, and particularly if there is someone who is already willing to take on the task of personally caring for the children, you may want to set up a trust to ensure the financial well-being of your children. The trustee may be an adult person, a surviving spouse, an older brother or sister, an aunt or uncle or other relative, a close personal friend, or, in quite substantial estates, a national bank.

A trustee may be given as broad powers as you think appropriate. If the trustee is a person you trust (and you wouldn't appoint one in the first place if you didn't) then it is usually recommended that the trustee have broad powers to administer the estate, using his or her best judgment. This happens because it is impossible to look into the future and predict what the situation of the children might be several years hence and what the economics of the times might dictate in handling the investments and making expenditures for the children.

Washington state statutes establish broad guidelines for handling a trust, accounting for all funds, and acting as a trustee. Any trustee would benefit from the services of a competent lawyer. It is hard enough for a layperson to be a competent trustee without expecting him or her to be familiar with the various laws with which he or she must comply.

3. A family trust

A second principal type of trust is one that will provide some additional income for your surviving spouse and then pass the principal of the trust on to your children, or perhaps to a charity. This type is usually called a "family" trust and has numerous useful purposes.

Briefly, the way it works in the case of a married couple is as follows: one-half of the community estate belongs to the survivor. The other one-half is left in trust, with all or a designed portion of the income going to the surviving spouse, and perhaps with a limited power in the trustee to invade (spend or encroach upon) the principal of the estate if needed for the care of the spouse. On the death of the surviving spouse, all of the principal goes to the children of the parties either directly or continued in a trust for the children.

You would be well-advised to set up a trust if you think that —

(a) your spouse is really not competent to handle the financial affairs with which he or she will be left, or

(b) the one-half of the estate your surviving spouse will have, plus the income from your half with a limited right to spend the principal, will be adequate to care for your spouse, or

(c) for tax purposes.

In general, if there is a substantial question of whether or not the survivor will have adequate funds, as stated above, then all of the money should be left to the surviving spouse, to be used as he or she sees fit. In that way he or she does not have to worry about trust management (i.e., when to spend the principal without destroying the trust) and all of the rest of the intricacies of a trust.

Provisions may be made for the use of a trustee other than the survivor to invade the principal in an unlimited amount if need be, but if there is any thought that it might well be necessary to spend all of the trust money, then there is little point in having a trust in the first place.

However, given an adequate amount of money, this type of trust may well be appropriate in your case, especially if you are interested in passing along to the children as much as possible, for this is a trust that can result in a substantial saving of the taxes which would come out of the portion that the children would ultimately receive. Here is the way the trust works.

Take a community estate of $1,200,000 (disregarding probate costs). Upon the death of Tom Testator, his wife owns one-half, or $600,000. Tom's $600,000 goes to the trust, and the *income* from this trust goes to the wife, together with as much of the principal as she needs (or use of the principal may be limited in amount or to a percentage of the whole).

On the death of the wife, the trust estate goes to the ultimate beneficiary of the trust. This may provide for some tax savings on the second death because it breaks a large estate into two halves. The first half is taxed on the husband's death and the second half on the wife's death.

If left outright to his wife as a marital deduction, Tom's estate would pay no tax; however, at the death of his wife, their combined estates would be taxed as the estate of the wife and, like most taxes, the higher the amount, the higher the tax bracket.

Now then, assume that no trust was established in Tom's will. This is what would happen to the estates of the parties. On Tom's death, one-half of the estate belongs to his wife; the one-half belonging to Tom is subject to taxation, and after taxes are paid the remainder goes to his wife. When Tom's wife dies, the portion left by her is subject to taxation, and the portion left by Tom is again subject to the payment of estate taxes.

You can see that, in this case, a trust would create substantial tax savings, but this savings is enjoyed by the children after both you and your spouse have died.

For the management of the trust you must appoint a trustee. If your spouse has sufficient business acumen and responsibility to handle the money wisely, then he or she should be the trustee. If not, then you should select some responsible adult who would be willing to take on the job and who would be compatible with your spouse. If no such person is available, then a corporate trustee should be considered.

Samples of this type of "family" trust are shown in Samples #4 and #5. However, if you have enough money to consider this type of a trust, it may be very shortsighted of you to try to draw it up yourself and you should consult an attorney. It cannot be stressed too strongly that these types of trusts, which have important tax consequences, must not only be drawn properly, but must be administered in accordance with the law, or you will have wasted your efforts.

4. Trust for ne'er-do-well child

After the death of your spouse, or if your spouse is adequately cared for, you may decide that a portion of your estate should go into a trust for a son or daughter who isn't quite living up to expectations and whose ability to handle money may be seriously limited. For this, almost any reasonable limitations may be included in your will that sets up the trust.

Here again caution is advised that any such provisions not be made too onerous for the trustee to accomplish and not be entirely unreasonable. It is generally considered unwise for you to try to control your estate from the grave for too long a period of time, but the only legal limit is 21 years after the death of any living person you name. However, if yours is the proper case, then here are a few suggestions from a wide range of possibilities:

> I direct that my Trustee shall pay to or for the benefit of my son all necessary expenses of his education, so long as he is actively pursuing a course of instruction leading to a degree in a Washington state college or university; such education expenses shall include tuition, lab fees, books, incidental scholastic fees, and board and room at the institution, or, if not living on campus, then a comparable payment may be made to my son which shall be approximately equal to that which would be required by a college dormitory for board and room. When my son receives his degree from a university, my Trustee shall thereupon pay to him one-third (⅓) of the net assets of the then remaining trust estate; when my son attains the age of thirty (30) years, my Trustee shall pay him one-half (½) of the then remaining assets of the trust estate; and my Trustee shall pay to him the balance of said trust estate when my son attains the age of thirty-five (35) years; provided, however, if my said son fails to complete his course of education so that he does not receive a college degree by the time he has attained the age of thirty (30) years, then and in that event only, I direct that my Trustee pay all of the then remaining assets of the trust estate to (other relative, friends, charities, schools, etc.).

5. Trust for a pet

You could use the following clause to set up a trust fund to look after a favorite pet. However, you should realize that the instructions could be complied with by merely, for example, placing the animal in a kennel where it would be well fed, but not very happy. It is probably better to direct that the pet be given to someone who would appreciate it.

> My trustee shall set aside the sum of $________ and to keep the said sum invested and to use the income and capital or so much thereof as my Trustee considers advisable for the maintenance and welfare of my dog (cat, bird)...and to ensure that my pet is properly fed and given proper care for the period of 20 years from my death if my said dog shall so long live, any income not so used in any year to be added to the capital of the said sum and dealt with as part thereof, and upon the death of my said dog or upon the expiration of the said period whichever event shall first occur and said sum together with any accumulations of income shall form part of the residue of my estate and be distributed pursuant therewith.

1. WHAT TO DO WHEN YOU WANT TO CHANGE PART OF YOUR WILL

Particular clauses in a will, such as specific bequests, special provisions for one or more children, the appointment of an executor and others, frequently have to be changed because of the aging process of the heirs, changes of economic conditions, and changes in the prospective size of the estate.

When you want to change only one or two clauses in your will, you may do so without making a whole new will. All you do is add what is known as a "codicil," which is an addition to the will (see Sample #6). Such a codicil, while changing only a part of the will, nevertheless has to be executed (signed and witnessed) with all of the formalities of the will itself.

While the law does not demand that a codicil be attached to a last will and testament, it is highly advisable that this be

SAMPLE #4
TRUST FORM OF A WILL

LAST WILL AND TESTAMENT

of

Terence Testament

I, Terence Testament, of King County, Washington, declare this to be my Last Will and Testament, and I revoke all former Wills and Codicils made by me.

FIRST

At the time of the execution of this, my Last Will and Testament, I am married to Tabitha Testament, and we have two children, Dick and Jane.

SECOND

I nominate and appoint my wife, Tabitha Testament, as Executrix and Trustee of this, my Last Will and Testament. In the event my said wife should predecease me, or should for any reason whatsoever fail to qualify as such or, having qualified, should for any reason whatsoever fail to complete the administration of my estate, I then nominate and appoint Ernest Executor as Executor of my estate.

No bond shall be required of anyone herein named as Executrix or Executor or Trustee.

THIRD

I give and bequeath to my wife, Tabitha Testament, all of my right, title and interest in and to automobiles, personal effects, jewelry, and all furniture and household furnishings and equipment.

FOURTH

All of the rest, residue, and remainder of my estate, of every character, kind and description, real, personal and mixed, separate and community, wheresoever situated and howsoever and whensoever acquired, I give, devise and bequeath unto my Trustee above named, to be held by my Trustee, IN TRUST, NEVERTHELESS, upon the following terms and conditions:

(a) My Executrix and Trustee shall pay, commencing with the month of my death, all of the net income of my estate, monthly, to my wife for the duration of her life, to be used for the health, care and maintenance, support, comfort, and enjoyment of my wife. Upon the death of my wife, all of the assets remaining in said trust I give and bequeath to my children, in equal shares; provided, if not all of my children are living at that time, then the share of any deceased child shall go to the remaining of my

T.T. initials June 15, 9- date

children, and provided further that if none of my children is living at the time of the demise of my wife, then all of the assets of the trust shall go to the children of my deceased children, by right of representation.

(b) No person dealing with the Trustee shall be obliged to inquire as to the Trustee's powers or see to the application of any money or property delivered to my trustee.

(c) My Trustee may rely with acquittance on the advice of counsel. (This means he may not be sued by beneficiaries for doing something in reliance upon legal advice.)

(d) My Trustee shall have full power to manage the assets of the trust in the administration, investment, and distribution thereof, and may manage the same in the manner which individuals may manage like property owned by them free of any trust without authorization of court.

(e) My Trustee shall not have to comply with the Trustee's Accounting Act of the State of Washington.

(f) Power to invade principal.

FIFTH

It is my will, and I so direct, that after a decree of a court of competent jurisdiction has admitted this, my Last Will and Testament, to probate, and my Executrix or Executor has filed a true inventory of all of the property of my estate and given such notices as are required by law, a decree of solvency of my estate be entered, and that thereafter my estate shall be managed and settled by my Executrix or Executor as herein provided without the intervention of any court or courts, and that no other proceeding in any probate or other court whatsoever be taken in the matter of this, my Last Will and Testament.

IN WITNESS WHEREOF, I have hereunto set my hand this 15th day of June, 199—, at Seattle, King County, Washington.

Terence Testament
Terence Testament
(Testator)

TT initials

June 15, 9— date

STATE OF WASHINGTON

COUNTY OF KING

Cookie Cutter and Melba Toast, being first duly sworn, on oath depose and say:

SAMPLE #4 — Continued

That this affidavit is made by the attesting witnesses to the Last Will and Testament of Terence Testament, who executed the foregoing instrument, consisting of two typewritten pages, on June 15, 199—, in the presence of each of us, and who did thereupon publish and declare the same to be his Last Will and Testament, and we, the undersigned, at his request and in his presence, and in the presence of each other, hereunto subscribed our names as witnesses thereto. That said Testator, at the time of executing said Will, was over the age of 18 years and appeared to be of sound mind and acting freely and voluntarily, without any duress or undue influence whatsoever. That we are competent and over the age of 18 years.

Cookie Cutter residing at Seattle, Washington

Melba Toast residing at Seattle, Washington

SUBSCRIBED AND SWORN to before me this 15th day of June, 199—.

Nathan Notary
NOTARY PUBLIC in and for
the State of Washington,
residing at Seattle.

The foregoing instrument, consisting of two typewritten pages, of which this is the last, was on the date thereof signed, initialed, and published by Terence Testament, who, at said time, appeared to be of sound and disposing mind and memory, and was by him declared to be his Last Will and Testament, in the presence of us, who, at his request and in his presence and in the presence of each other, have hereunto set out hands as witnesses thereto this 15th day of June, 199 —. Each page of this Will bears the signature of the Testator.

Cookie Cutter residing at Seattle, Washington

Melba Toast residing at Seattle, Washington

TT initials June 15, 9– date

SAMPLE #5
ALTERNATE TRUST FORM FOR A WILL

LAST WILL AND TESTAMENT

of

Sally Sunshine

I, Sally Sunshine, of King County, Washington, declare this to be my Last Will and Testament, and I revoke all former Wills and Codicils made by me.

FIRST

At the time of the execution of this, my Last Will and Testament, I am married to Stan Sunshine. I have two children, Summer, aged 15, and Ray, aged 11. I shall hereinafter refer to my husband and children by their given names.

SECOND

I nominate and appoint my husband, Stan Sunshine, as the Executor and Trustee of this, my Last Will and Testament. In the event my husband should predecease me, or should for any reason whatsoever fail to qualify as such or, having qualified, should for any reason whatsoever fail to complete the administration of my estate, I then nominate and appoint Tom Trustworthy as Executor and Trustee of my estate.

No bond shall be required of anyone herein named as Executrix, Executor, or Trustee.

THIRD

I give and bequeath to my beloved husband, Stan Sunshine, all of my interest in our home furnishings, equipment, and other usual contents of our home, and automobiles which we may own, together with all of my personal effects, and (here set forth what, if any, of the balance of your estate you wish to go to your husband).

FOURTH

All of my estate (or the residue of my estate) or ($20,000) or (one-half of my estate) or (any other reasonable variation which will provide funds for your intended purpose), I give, devise, and bequeath to my Trustee named, IN TRUST, NEVERTHELESS, for the following uses and purposes:

(a) To provide for the care, education, and maintenance of my two children, Summer, aged 15, and Ray, aged 11. It is my intention that my children shall be provided for insofar as the funds in the

SS initials July 15, 9– date

trust are adequate in the manner in which they have been accustomed to enjoy. With respect to education, my Trustee shall include within that term necessary expenditures of any school of higher education, including board and room thereat if the school is located outside of the City of Seattle. My Trustee shall at all times consider whatever other resources are available to my two said children.

(b) When Summer shall attain the age of twenty-two (22) years, the then remaining trust estate shall be divided in two portions, and one-half thereof shall be given to my said daughter, Summer.

(c) The trust shall thereafter continue for the use of my son, Ray, as aforesaid; provided, that when Ray attains the age of twenty-two (22) years, all of the funds remaining in said trust shall be delivered to Ray, and the trust shall end.

(d) If either of my children shall fail to survive until the age of twenty-two (22) years, then upon the demise of one, all of the trust estate shall be used for the benefit of the other and shall be paid to him or her upon attaining the age of twenty-two (22) years; provided, that if neither of my children survive to the age of twenty-two (22) years, then my Trustee shall, upon the demise of the second of my two children, pay over all of the funds remaining in the trust estate to such charitable organization as my Trustee may select, which organization should, if possible, be related to the events which caused the demise of either or both of my said two children.

FIFTH

My Trustee may rely with acquittance on advice of counsel on questions of law.

SIXTH

The beneficial interest of any beneficiary shall not be subject to claims of the respective beneficiary's creditors or others, nor to legal process, and shall not be voluntarily or involuntarily assigned, alienated, or encumbered. (This clause will prevent the beneficiary from assigning any of the trust assets for debts or any other purpose and will likewise prevent a creditor from attaching any of the assets.)

SEVENTH

My Trustee shall have all of the rights, powers, and duties given by law on the date hereof, including those set forth in the Washington Trust Act as amended.

SS initials July 15, 9- date

EIGHTH

It is my will, and I so direct, that after a decree of a court of competent jurisdiction has admitted this, my Last Will and Testament, to probate, and my Executrix or Executor has filed a true inventory of all of the property of my estate and given such notices as are required by law, a decree of solvency of my estate be entered, and that thereafter my estate shall be managed and settled by my Executrix or Executor as herein provided without the intervention of any court or courts as provided by the State of Washington, and that no other proceeding in any probate or other court whatsoever be taken into the matter of this, my Last Will and Testament.

IN WITNESS WHEREOF, I have hereunto set my hand this 15th day of July 199—, at Seattle, King County, Washington.

Sally Sunshine
Sally Sunshine
(Testatrix)

STATE OF WASHINGTON

COUNTY OF KING

Walter Witness and Wesley Witness, being first duly sworn, on oath depose and say:

That this affidavit is made by the attesting witnesses to the Last Will and Testament of Sally Sunshine, who executed the foregoing instrument, consisting of three pages, on the 15th day of July, 199__, in the presence of each of us, and who did thereupon publish and declare the same to be her Last Will and Testament, and we, the undersigned, at her request and in her presence, and in the presence of each other, hereunto subscribed our names as witnesses thereto. That said Testatrix at the time of executing said Will, was over the age of 18 years and appeared to be of sound mind and acting freely

SS initials July 15, 9– date

SAMPLE #5 — Continued

and voluntarily, without any duress or undue influence whatsoever. That we are competent and over the age of 18 years.

Walter Witness residing at Seattle, Washington

Wesley Witness residing at Seattle, Washington

SUBSCRIBED AND SWORN to before me this 15th day of July, 199—.

Nathan Notary
NOTARY PUBLIC in and for
the State of Washington,
residing at Seattle.

The foregoing instrument, consisting of three typewritten pages, of which this is the last, was on the date thereof signed, initialed, and published by Sally Sunshine, who, at said time, appeared to be of sound and disposing mind and memory, and was by him declared to be his Last Will and Testament, in the presence of us, who, at his request and in his presence and in the presence of each other, have hereunto set out hands as witnesses thereto this 15th day of June, 199 —. Each page of this Will bears the signature of the Testator.

Walter Witness residing at Seattle, Washington

Wesley Witness residing at Seattle, Washington

SS initials *July 15, 9-* date

done. To keep them separate is to risk one part not being found when needed.

You are advised to check your will every few years and revise it, if necessary.

m. SUMMARY OF STEPS TO MAKE A WILL

After reading the foregoing and looking at the sample, you should now be prepared to begin drafting your own will.

First, sit down and make a complete inventory of all your assets — cash, stocks, bonds, money due you, real and personal property of all kinds. Then list your immediate family and also other relatives and friends whom you might want to remember as beneficiaries or alternative beneficiaries.

Next, write down how you want your property distributed upon your death. For the actual drafting, keep these important steps in mind:

(a) First, set forth the introductory statement to the effect that you are hereby making and executing your last will and testament.

(b) Revoke the old will, if any.

(c) List the name of your spouse and the names and ages of all your children, natural and adopted, and whether you want to leave them anything or not.

(d) Name the executor and an alternative executor.

(e) Set forth in clear language the exact manner you wish your estate to be distributed. Check over the samples and reread the suggested alternative clauses. You may wish to use the publisher's will and estate planning kit, *Have You Made Your Will?*, at this stage.

(f) Sign the will in the presence of two competent, adult witnesses — tell them the document is your will and ask them to sign. Remember, no beneficiaries should be witnesses as they will not receive their bequests.

SAMPLE #6
CODICIL

CODICIL TO LAST WILL AND TESTAMENT
of
Tom Testator

I, Tom Testator, of King County, Washington, being of sound and disposing mind and memory, and acting freely and voluntarily, do hereby make, publish, and declare this to be the first codicil to my Last Will and Testament executed on January 1, 199—.

FIRST

To paragraph 5, commencing on page 1 of my Last Will and Testament, there shall be added a new paragraph number 5(c), reading as follows:

To my friend, Perry Poorhouse, of Debtorsville, Washington, the sum of One Thousand Dollars ($1,000).

SECOND

Subparagraph (d) of paragraph 7 on page 3 of said Last Will and Testament, referring to John Doe, of Seattle, Washington, be and the same is hereby deleted in its entirety and the bequest therein contained shall lapse and become part of the residue of my estate.

THIRD

Paragraph 6 of my said Last Will and Testament is hereby deleted in its entirety, and the following is hereby substituted therefor:

I hereby nominate and appoint as Executor of this, my Last Will and Testament, my friend, Ernest Executor, to serve as such without being required to give bond of any sort whatsoever and without the intervention of court as provided by the laws of the state of Washington.

Other than as herein specifically set forth, I hereby confirm and republish my Last Will and Testament referred to above.

IN WITNESS WHEREOF, I have hereunto set my hand and seal at Seattle, King County, Washington, on January 30, 199—.

Tom Testator
(Testator)

TT initials Jan. 30, 9– date

SAMPLE #6 — Continued

STATE OF WASHINGTON

COUNTY OF KING

Walter Witness and Wesley Witness, being first duly sworn, on oath depose and say:

That this affidavit is made by the attesting witnesses to the first Codicil to the Last Will and Testament of Tom Testator, who executed the foregoing instrument, consisting of one page, on January 30, 199—, in the presence of each of us, and who did thereupon publish and declare the same to be the first Codicil to his Last Will and Testament, and we, the undersigned, at his request and in his presence, and in the presence of each other, hereunto subscribed our names as witnesses thereto. That said Testator, at the time of executing said Codicil, was over the age of 18 years and appeared to be of sound mind and acting freely and voluntarily, without any duress or undue influence whatsoever. That we are competent and over the age of 18 years.

Walter Witness residing at Seattle, Washington

Wesley Witness residing at Seattle, Washington

SUBSCRIBED AND SWORN to before me this 30th day of January, 199—.

Nathan Notary
NOTARY PUBLIC in and for
the State of Washington,
residing at Seattle.

The foregoing instrument, consisting of two typewritten pages, of which this is the last, was on the date thereof signed, initialed, and published by Tom Testator, who, at said time, appeared to be of sound and disposing mind and memory, and was by him declared to be the first codicil to the Last Will and Testament of Tom Testator, in the presence of us, who, at his request and in his presence and in the presence of each other, have hereunto set out hands as witnesses thereto this 30th day of January, 199 —. Each page of this Will bears the signature of the Testator.

Walter Witness residing at Seattle, Washington

Wesley Witness residing at Seattle, Washington

TT initials Jan 30, 9- date

(f) Sign the will in the presence of two competent, adult witnesses — tell them the document is your will and ask them to sign. Remember, no beneficiaries should be witnesses as they will not receive their bequests. When you use the affidavit form, do the foregoing before a notary public. The notary should put the witnesses under oath and then sign and seal the document. Almost all lawyers are notaries, and most real estate offices and banks have at least one notary. They are also listed in the telephone book under "Notaries, Public."

(g) Put your will in a safe place and tell your executor where it is.

n. WHERE SHOULD YOU KEEP YOUR WILL?

Your will and your community property agreement, if you have one, are valuable papers and should be kept in a safe place that is as fireproof as possible. Recommended places are a home safe, a strong box, in a plastic bag in a freezer, or a safe deposit box. Be aware that there may be problems with the safe deposit if the key cannot be found or the bank will not let a person other than the testator open the box.

If you had the assistance of a lawyer, you might consider leaving the original in the office's will file and taking with you only a copy which could be kept in any convenient place where you are able to refer to it from time to time. However, if you do that, let the lawyer know if you move or if there is any change in your family or in your assets which might dictate a change in your will.

If you prepare a new will on your own, or with the guidance of a different lawyer, tell the first lawyer to destroy your old will.

3
COMMUNITY PROPERTY AGREEMENTS

The state of Washington is unique in the United States for its provision of another method of passing property upon death. A statute, RCW 26.16.120 (Revised Code of Washington), provides as follows:

> **Agreements as to status.** Nothing contained in any of the provisions of this chapter or in any law of this state, shall prevent the husband and wife from jointly entering into any agreement concerning the status or disposition of the whole or any portion of the community property, then owned by them or afterwards to be acquired, to take effect upon the death of either. But such agreement may be made at any time by the husband and wife by the execution of an instrument in writing under their hands and seals, and to be witnessed, acknowledged and certified in the same manner as deeds to real estate are required to be, under the laws of the state, and the same may at any time thereafter be altered or amended in the same manner: Provided, however, that such agreement shall not derogate from the right of creditors, nor be construed to curtail the powers of the superior court to set aside or cancel such agreements for fraud or under some other recognized head of equity jurisdiction, at the suit of either party.

The agreement authorized by this statutory provision is generally called a "community property agreement." By means of this agreement the estate of a deceased person who has transferred ownership of his or her property need not be "probated." This eliminates the cost and delay of probate and is the chief advantage of the community property agreement. There are, however, disadvantages, which will be discussed later.

a. WHO CAN UTILIZE A COMMUNITY PROPERTY AGREEMENT?

A community property agreement is a contract or a legally binding and enforceable agreement in which the parties may agree on the ownership of all or part of the property owned by them individually or together and, in addition, may agree that the survivor of them shall own the whole upon the death of the other.

Not everyone may enter into a community property agreement. The statute authorizing community property agreements strictly limits the availability of this method of transferring property to married couples only.

b. WHAT CAN THE COMMUNITY PROPERTY AGREEMENT ACCOMPLISH?

The courts of this state have interpreted the community property agreement statute to mean that married couples may contract with each other as follows:

1. Agreements effective as of death of first spouse

Couples may agree that all property owned by them, both community and separate, as of the death of either of them, will be deemed to be community property and will be the sole and separate property of the surviving spouse. The community property agreement shown in Sample #7 is an example of this type of community property agreement.

2. Agreements effective as of date of agreement

It is not necessary that the parties to a community property agreement draft the agreement in such a way that it is effective only upon the death of one of the parties. The agreement may provide that all separate property is converted and is deemed to be community property as of the date of the agreement. However, this may cause problems in the event of a dissolution.

The agreement may also provide that all property acquired after the agreement is made, regardless of its source and regardless of whether it would otherwise be separate property, will also be community property. In this case, separate property is immediately transferred into community property. Later, all of the property of the parties becomes the sole and separate property of the surviving spouse when the first spouse dies. (See Sample #8.)

In summing up, by virtue of the authority conferred on married couples by RCW 26.16.120, as interpreted by various court cases, a community property agreement can change the ownership (status) of property from separate property to community property as of the date of the agreement.

The agreement can also effect the same change in the status of property that has not yet been acquired by the date of the agreement.

Similarly, although it is far less common, a married couple may contract to change the status of property from community property to separate property. Again, a contract of this type can affect property acquired later than the date of the agreement in the same manner it affects property already owned by the parties as of the date of the agreement.

Although the language of RCW 26.16.120, together with various court cases construing that statute, imply more variations in the use of community property agreements than those set out above, including the disposition of property involving third persons operating in conjunction with the will of one of the contracting parties, it is my belief that you should consider only those types of community property agreements that have

SAMPLE #7
COMMUNITY PROPERTY AGREEMENT CHANGING THE STATUS OF PROPERTY AT DEATH

COMMUNITY PROPERTY SURVIVORSHIP AGREEMENT

THIS AGREEMENT is made and entered into this 16th day of July, 199—, by and between Mary L. Bliss and Marty L. Bliss, husband and wife, pursuant to the statutes of the state of Washington in such case made and provided, for the purpose of establishing the status of all property owned by the parties upon the demise of either;

NOW, THEREFORE, in consideration of the promises of each to the other, and also in consideration of the love and affection that each bears to the other, it is hereby mutually agreed:

That upon the death of either of them, but not prior to such death, all property, real, personal, and mixed, of whatsoever kind or nature, owned by the parties, and whether originally acquired as separate property or community property, and all property hereafter acquired by the parties from any source whatsoever, shall be considered as community property and shall, upon such death, immediately become the sole property of the survivor of them.

IN WITNESS WHEREOF, the parties hereto have hereunto set their hands this 16th day of July, 199—.

Marty L. Bliss
MARTY L. BLISS

Mary L. Bliss
MARY L. BLISS

STATE OF WASHINGTON

COUNTY OF KING

On this 16th day of July, 199—, personally appeared before me Mary L. Bliss and Marty L. Bliss, to me known to be the individuals described in and who executed the foregoing instrument, and they acknowledged to me that they signed the same as their free and voluntary act and deed for the uses and purposes therein mentioned.

IN WITNESS WHEREOF, I have hereunto set my hand and affixed my official seal the day and year above written.

I. M. Witness
NOTARY PUBLIC in and for
the State of Washington,
residing at Seattle.

SAMPLE #8
COMMUNITY PROPERTY AGREEMENT CHANGING THE STATUS OF PROPERTY AS OF THE DATE OF THE AGREEMENT

COMMUNITY PROPERTY AGREEMENT

THIS AGREEMENT is made and entered into this 25th day of May, 199—, by and between Sally Spouse and Sol Spouse, husband and wife, pursuant to the statutes of the state of Washington in such case made and provided, for the purpose of establishing the status of all property owned by the parties upon the demise of either;

NOW, THEREFORE, in consideration of the promises of each to the other, and also in consideration of the love and affection that each bears to the other, it is hereby mutually agreed:

I.

That all property, real, personal, and mixed, of whatsoever kind or nature, owned by the parties, or to which they may be entitled, and whether originally acquired as separate property or community property, and all property hereafter acquired by the parties in any manner whatsoever, is hereby declared henceforth to be community property owned entirely by the community composed of these parties, and it is agreed that neither party shall hereafter own any separate property or separate interest in any property of whatsoever kind or nature.

II.

That in the event of the death of the said Sol Spouse (husband) while the said Sally Spouse (wife) survives, then the whole of all property, of every kind, nature, or description, now owned or hereafter to be acquired by the parties, shall at once vest in the said Sally Spouse (wife) in fee simple.

III.

That in the event of the death of the said Sally Spouse (wife) while the said Sol Spouse (husband) survives, then the whole of all property, of every kind nature, or description, now owned or hereafter to be acquired by the parties, shall at once vest in the said Sol Spouse (husband) in fee simple.

SAMPLE #8 — Continued

IN WITNESS WHEREOF, the parties have hereunto set their hands and seals the day and year first above written.

Sol Spouse
SOL SPOUSE

Sally Sanderson
SALLY SPOUSE

STATE OF WASHINGTON

COUNTY OF KING

THIS IS TO CERTIFY that before me, the undersigned, a notary public in and for the state of Washington, duly commissioned and sworn, personally appeared Sol Spouse and Sally Spouse, to me known to be the individuals described in and who executed the foregoing instrument, and they acknowledged to me that they signed and sealed the same as their free and voluntary act and deed, for the uses and purposes therein mentioned.

IN WITNESS WHEREOF, I have hereunto set my hand and official seal this 25th day of May, 199—.

I. M. Notary
NOTARY PUBLIC in and for
the State of Washington,
residing at Seattle.

been accepted and approved by the courts and are therefore unquestionably effective.

c. WHAT ARE THE DISADVANTAGES OF A COMMUNITY PROPERTY AGREEMENT?

(a) A community property agreement may not include anyone other than a spouse; it cannot be a trust for any purpose. It is not revocable unless both spouses agree and act together to revoke it. Thus a very real problem may arise if one spouse wishes to alter or abolish the agreement and the other one does not (for example, one spouse decides that he or she would like some third person, and not the other spouse, to have his or her property upon death). Problems also arise if the spouses decide to dissolve their marriage. If one spouse feels that the community property agreement was or is inequitable, that spouse may petition the court to set it aside. A will, on the other hand, may be changed by the testator alone at any time.

(b) If the deceased managed the community property, or perhaps operated a business, he or she may have left debts about which the survivor knows nothing. Creditors may appear for up to six years later and legally demand payment.

On the other hand, if a will is probated in the usual manner, a published notice to creditors is given. If a creditor does not file a claim within four months, the claim is forever barred.

(c) Only a will may provide for alternative beneficiaries if husband and wife die in a common disaster. For this reason, among others, it is recommended that couples have a will even if they also have a community property agreement.

(d) If separate property is converted to community property prior to death, it may be subject to some community property obligations which might otherwise have been avoided.

(e) As stated earlier, if a couple executes a community property agreement and then become involved in a dissolution, the agreement will drastically affect the distribution of property since it has changed the character of what once was separate property.

d. WHAT ARE THE ADVANTAGES OF A COMMUNITY PROPERTY AGREEMENT?

(a) It is easily understood. It is a simple contract between husband and wife.

(b) On the first death, the agreement is usually recorded in the recorder's office in the county of residence. If the parties own real estate in other countries, copies must be recorded there also.

(c) There is no probate. If any federal estate tax is payable, fill out the federal tax return, and pay the computed tax. Then, from the tables provided in the federal instruction sheet compute the Washington state estate or pickup tax and send that to Olympia. When you receive tax clearances from both the IRS and from Olympia, record the releases in the county office where the deeds are recorded.

e. HOW TO MAKE LEGALLY ENFORCEABLE PROPERTY AGREEMENTS

1. Requisites of the agreement

In order to be binding and enforceable, a community property agreement must —

(a) be in writing,

(b) be voluntarily and knowingly executed by both parties to the agreement,

(c) fully and accurately list all property of the parties (in the case of pre-marital agreements), and

(d) be signed and acknowledged in the same manner as a deed is. That is to say, the agreement must be executed by both parties in the presence of a notary public, who then acknowledges their signatures.

2. Recording

Recording is not necessary for you to have an effective community property agreement. Nevertheless, if the community property agreement in question is intended to be binding upon the parties and on the public it should be recorded.

If a community property agreement transfers an interest in real property, it is in the nature of a deed and it *must* be recorded in the county where the property is located. Public recording of a document indicating an interest in real property, whether it is in a deed, mortgage, or community property agreement, is the way an individual gives notice to any interested parties that he or she is the owner of or has an interest in the described property. These are the records title companies use to secure their information and issue policies guaranteeing title to property when it is sold.

To record, present the agreement to the clerk of the county auditor's office, the county recorder's office, or the office of records and elections, which are several of the different names used by the various counties in Washington. The office where the recording function is handled is located in the county court house or adjacent building. You can find the proper county office by looking under the "County" listing in the appropriate telephone directory.

You must record the agreement in the county where the real property is located. If the real property is located in more than one county, or if the document refers to more than one parcel of real property located in different counties, you must do your recording in each county that real property is located in.

Since there is only one agreement, record it in the county of the deceased first. When it is returned to you, send it to the next county and, in turn, to as many counties as necessary. The recording date and time in each county will show on the face of the agreement. When the document is returned, file it for safekeeping among your valuable papers.

If the original agreement, after having been recorded as above, is lost, you will always be able to get a certified copy of it from any county where it was recorded. A fee is required for recording documents.

f. WHAT HAPPENS IF THERE IS BOTH AN AGREEMENT AND A WILL?

Many lawyers have married couples make wills and a community property agreement. Upon the death of one spouse, the survivor may then proceed under the will or under the community property agreement, whichever appears to be more advantageous with regard to the various expenses, including taxes, associated with distribution of the assets of the estate.

Whether it is more advantageous to distribute the estate through probating the estate or through the community property agreement depends on several factors.

First, as already mentioned, is the size of the estate. A larger estate may have to be distributed by probating the estate because of the tax advantages of setting up a trust.

The existence of creditors may also be a factor to be considered in making this choice. As already discussed, when an estate is probated, all creditors must notify the personal representative in writing of their claims within four months of the date of the first publication of a notice to creditors.

On the other hand, if the community property agreement is used to distribute the property, and there is no court case pending and no notice is given to creditors, creditors have up to six years to bring an action for the recovery of the amount owed, depending, of course, on the debt involved.

Furthermore, it is not uncommon for couples to sign a community property agreement many years prior to the death of the first spouse at a time when their estate is minimal and when the community property agreement would be the appropriate method of disposing of the estate of the deceased spouse. However, as time passes, the couple may prosper, and the assets of the estate accumulate so that it is preferable to use the will instead of the community property agreement, because of the facts mentioned above.

Where both wills and a community property agreement exist, it is often preferred that the community property agreement not be recorded until the death of the first spouse, if at all. The recording of the community property agreement has the effect of giving public notice of its existence. In the absence of this type of public notice, the surviving spouse is free to ignore the agreement and proceed under the will.

However, the practice of not recording the community property agreement until the death of the first spouse could be detrimental to the interests of the surviving spouse.

For instance, assume that one spouse owns separate property. If the community property agreement is of the type that changes separate property to community property on the date of the agreement, and later one of the spouses, unknown to the other, sells property which, were it not for the agreement, would be his or her separate property, it is possible that the sale to a third person would be valid and that the surviving spouse could be deprived of his or her interest in the property. If the agreement were recorded immediately after it was signed, the interest of the surviving spouse would in all probability be protected.

This is because title search and issuance of a title insurance policy is a necessary part of almost all sales of real property in the state of Washington. Any prospective purchaser would, therefore, become aware of the existence of the community property agreement affecting the property. Under those circumstances, the prospective purchaser would refuse to purchase the property without a deed from both spouses.

One advantage of having a community property agreement that changes separate property to community property as of the date of the agreement, assuming it is recorded, is that all the property of the parties, both separate and community, is consolidated in the form of community property. Neither spouse retains any individual or separate property.

Under the laws of the state of Washington real property that is community property can only be transferred or sold to third persons upon the written signature of both spouses. By making all property community property a couple will ensure that all the property will be preserved until the time of death of the first spouse, unless both spouses agree to sell the property and have signed the necessary documents.

On the other hand, one spouse may desire the other spouse to inherit his or her property on death, but may not wish to give up control over the property while he or she is alive. In this situation, the couple may decide to enter into an agreement that will be effective only upon the death of one.

Previous editions of this book suggested that the time of recording a community property agreement might be affected by tax considerations. However, the federal unlimited "marital deduction" means that one marital partner may now give to the other assets of any value either as a gift while both are living or upon the death of one. Also, there is no longer a state inheritance tax, so there are no tax reasons for not recording the agreement. Of course, in a large estate, tax liability on the death of the surviving spouse could well dictate the need for estate planning.

g. CONCLUSION

In appropriate circumstances, notably where the size of the estate is minimal and you and your spouse wish all your property upon the death of one of you to go to the other, signing a properly drafted community property agreement may be advisable.

However, there are problems associated with a community property agreement (especially if a dissolution later occurs); if you have any doubt about the advisability of making such an agreement, you should first consult your attorney. Finally, no taxes are avoided or saved with a community property agreement.

4
BENEFITS NOT PASSING UNDER THE WILL

This is the shortest chapter in the book, but not the least important.

Many people feel that as soon as they have prepared and signed their will or community property agreement, their entire estate is taken care of. Not necessarily so. At various times after preparing your will, you might sign or be part of numerous things that affect your estate. But a new will will have no effect whatsoever on many of these documents or arrangements.

A good example of this is joint tenancy, and the most common form of joint tenancy found in the state of Washington is in various types of bank or savings association accounts. All such institutions have signature cards you sign when you open an account. You may have had someone else sign the signature card with you.

If you and another sign a signature card that has wording on it to the effect that it is an agreement for "joint tenancy with right of survivorship," then if you die while the agreement is in effect, all of the proceeds of that account will immediately become the property of the other signatory to the card. Neither your community property agreement nor your will can control the account.

Another common oversight is with insurance policies. If your estate is subject to an estate tax, no insurance policy should be made payable to the estate if there is any other possible beneficiary. However, an insurance policy payable to the executor may be appropriate if it appears that the estate will "lack liquidity," i.e., if it consists almost entirely of real or tangible personal property and there are insufficient cash assets or securities readily convertible into cash to pay the expenses of the probate. For this kind of estate, your insurance agent can help you to secure a policy that will serve your needs well and prevent problems in the processing of your estate. The naming of one or more proper insurance beneficiaries is an important part of estate planning.

You can avoid having some of your property pass under your will by giving it away while you are still alive. Give a painting or furniture or silver — anything you don't need or use any more — to someone you know would enjoy it. Your extra stocks, bonds, or cash could provide a longed-for vacation or education for someone in your family. Remember, the tax laws now allow you to give away up to $10,000 a year to as many people as you wish.

Many employer benefit or retirement plans are payable on death to a named beneficiary. These, too, are usually unaffected by your will. Also, there are various types of contracts involving bonds, mortgages, notes, trust agreements, etc., that might contain agreements as to the disposition of assets upon your death. So, when you review your estate with final disposition in mind, don't overlook any area in which you have an interest.

The will and estate planning kit *Have You Made Your Will?*, published by Self-Counsel Press, includes forms for drafting your own will and planning your estate. The estate planning forms also list the areas you should remember when reviewing your estate.

APPENDIX
SPECIAL SITUATION CLAUSES

1. Guardian

"If my wife should predecease me or die prior to the completion of the probate of my estate, then in that event only I nominate and appoint as guardian of my children above-named my sister, Maria, or if she is unable or unwilling to serve in that capacity, then my brother, Joseph."

2. Personal effects

"To my wife I give all my personal effects and all of my interest in and to all of our household furniture, equipment, and incidentals, and any automobiles which we may own at the time of my death. The foregoing is limited to tangible personal property. In the event that my wife should predecease me or fail to survive me by thirty (30) days, then and in that event only I give all of such items to my children in equal shares as nearly as said items may be apportioned by the children themselves, but if they are unable to agree, then the apportionment shall be at the exclusive discretion of my Executor."

3. Forgiveness of debt

"I release Harry Happy from and against any indebtedness to me or my estate at the time of my death or thereafter. Should any such indebtedness be secured by mortgage or other charge I direct my Trustee to execute a full release and discharge of the same and of all claims thereunder."

4. Specific bequests

"To my son, John, I leave all of my shop equipment and tools, including but not limited to my table saw, my hand power tools, saws, screwdrivers, hammers, wrenches, and other tools located in my shop."

"To my friend, Emily Welsch, I give my Whittier seascape painting."

"To my friend, Ralph Johnson, I leave my office desk and chair."

"To my neighbor and friend, Nelson Neighbor, I leave my riding lawnmower and such other lawn-care equipment as he may select."

"To my son, John, my shares in Bigshot Company Inc. If at my death the said shares as the result of any stock dividend, stock split, amalgamation, reconstruction or rearrangement of capital of the said company, or the sale of its undertaking to any other company shall be represented by a different capital holding either in the said company or in any other company to which I am entitled at my death, then the said bequest shall take effect as if it had been a bequest of the capital holding or holdings which as the result of such stock dividend, stock split, amalgamation, reconstruction or rearrangement or sale took the place of such shares."

5. Percentage bequests

"I direct that my estate shall be reduced to cash, and that all of the net proceeds thereof shall be paid as follows:

(a) 33⅓% thereof to my sister, Ethel.

(b) 10% thereof to my friends, Marian and George Smith.

(c) 10% thereof to my Uncle Abraham.

(d) 10% thereof to the Millionaire Club Charity.

(e) The balance thereof to the Westheaven Presbyterian Church.

Should any of the foregoing individuals fail to survive me, then the amounts allotted to them shall go to their children, if any, and if no children, then to their spouses; but if they leave neither children nor spouse, then anything left to the said individuals shall go in equal shares to the Millionaire Club Charity and the Westheaven Presbyterian Church."

GLOSSARY

ADMINISTRATOR
Person appointed by the courts to be the personal representative of someone who dies without a will (feminine form: administratrix)

AFFIDAVIT
Sworn statement in writing, made before an authorized officer (e.g., the witnesses who sign the attestation clause will have to make an affidavit after the testator/testatrix dies, unless their affidavits are included in the testator's or testatrix's will)

APPOINT
To name someone who is to perform a task

ASSETS
Property of a deceased person subject by law to payment of his or her debts and legacies

ATTESTATION CLAUSE
Clause in a will that follows the signature of the testator/testatrix and offers proof, evidence, or affirmation that the testator/testatrix really did make the will and was able to do so

BENEFICIARY
Person who derives some benefit, whether money or property, from a will

BEQUEST
Legacy or gift of personal property given in a will

CLAUSE
Section, article, phrase, or paragraph containing a legal provision, direction, or arrangement

CODICIL
Amendment to a will, requiring all the formalities of execution of a will

COMMUNITY PROPERTY
Property acquired by a married couple, other than separate property

CREDITOR
Person to whom money is owed, and due

DEVISE
In a will, the leaving of real property

ESCHEAT
Process by which the assets of a deceased person pass to the state government when that person dies leaving no will, spouse, or next-of-kin

ESTATE
Everything the deceased owned

EXECUTOR
Person appointed in a will to administer the estate of the deceased (feminine form: executrix)

GUARDIAN
Person appointed by law to take care of the person or the affairs of a minor or someone unable to take care of himself or herself; a trustee, protector. May be guardian of person only or property only or both

GUARDIAN AD LITEM
Someone appointed to look after the legal interest of a legally incompetent individual during litigation or probate or for a specific purpose

INVADE
Term used to describe the act of spending the principal of a trust fund, along with the interest

JURISDICTION
Extent of authority

NOTARY
Public officer authorized to certify deeds and contracts, to record the fact that a certain person swears that something is true

OATH
Solemn affirmation of the truth of what is stated

PERSONAL PROPERTY
All property with the exception of real estate and buildings (also known as "personalty")

PERSONAL REPRESENTATIVE
Person administering an estate, whether he or she be an executor/executrix or an administrator/administratrix, or guardian

PROBATE
Official proof of a will; settlement of a deceased's estate

REAL PROPERTY
Land and buildings (also known as "real estate")

RESIDENCE
Where you make your home

RESIDUE
What is left after all specific bequests have been distributed

REVOKE
To cancel, to withdraw, to take back

SEPARATE PROPERTY
Property acquired before marriage or during marriage by inheritance or gift that is kept separate from the community property; also passive income from separate assets. **Note:** if labor is expended on separate assets after marriage, separate property may become partially or completely community property

SPECIFIC BEQUEST
Gift under a will of a specific item of personal property, or cash from an identifiable fund

SPECIFIC DEVISE
Gift under a will of a specific item of real property

OTHER TITLES FROM SELF-COUNSEL

PROBATE GUIDE FOR WASHINGTON

A step-by-step guide to probating an estate

by Phillip L. Thom, Attorney

$14.95

By using this book as a guide, you can probate an estate yourself and save thousands of dollars in legal fees. Probate is the legal process necessary for settling an estate. It sounds difficult, but it doesn't have to be. This book, written by a lawyer in simple, easy-to-understand language, explains the probate procedure in step-by-step detail. The sample forms show how to do all the required paper work for estates that do not have technical complications. Even if you are not planning to probate an estate, you will find the information in this book helpful in your discussions with your lawyer.

Some of the common questions answered in this book are:

- How can small estates be settled simply?
- Who can be a personal representative or executor?
- What taxes must be paid on an estate?
- What happens in court?
- How is the family supported during probate?
- How do you prove that a will is valid?
- What fees are involved in a probate?
- What are the rights of minors?

REAL ESTATE BUYING/SELLING GUIDE FOR WASHINGTON

Charles J. Covello, Attorney

$8.95

Buying or selling a house can be an exciting event in your life. But you may get more excitement than you bargained for unless you understand how a real estate transaction works in Washington. This book gives you a concise explanation of all the stages in a transaction and explains the responsibilities of the seller, buyer, agent, and lawyer.

It answers questions such as:

- How much should you spend on a house?
- What down payment is required?
- How do you arrange a mortgage?
- What are the pros and cons of FHA and VA financing?
- How can you use your home to save taxes?
- What is an earnest money agreement? How binding is it?
- How do you make a counteroffer?
- What happens when a mortgage is foreclosed? Can you save your home?
- What are the advantages of condominiums, cooperative apartments, and mobile homes?

FINANCIAL FREEDOM ON $5 A DAY:

A step-by-step strategy for small investors

Chuck Chakrapani, M.Sc., Ph.D.

$10.95

Even if you know nothing about investing, this book will show you how to achieve financial freedom starting with very little money. It explains how you can use investment strategies that most people think are available only to the rich. Also included is a valuable resource directory that gives the names and addresses of important contacts throughout North America.

Contents include:

- You can achieve financial freedom
- How to get money to invest
- Getting started
- How to get high interest
- How to invest in the stock market
- How to invest in bonds
- How to invest internationally
- How to invest in gold
- How to invest in silver
- Eight more ways to make money
- Three strategies for even higher profits
- How to get free information
- Fundamentals of financial growth
- A blueprint for financial freedom

ORDERING INFORMATION

All prices are subject to change without notice. Books are available in book, department, and stationery stores. If you cannot buy the book through a store, please use this order form.

Please send your order to:
Self-Counsel Press Inc.
1704 N. State Street
Bellingham, WA 98225

Name ______________________________

Address ______________________________

____

Charge to: ❑ Visa ❑ MasterCard

Account Number ______________________________
Validation Date ______________________________
Expiry Date ______________________________

Signature ______________________________

❑ Check here for free catalog.

YES, please send me
_____copies of **Have You Made Your Will?**, $5.95 (see chapter 2 for details)
_____copies of **Probate Guide for Washington**, $14.95
_____copies of **Probate Forms for Washington A** *(Full Probate)*, $14.95
_____copies of **Probate Forms for Washington B** *(Short Form of Probate)*, $5.95
_____copies of **Marriage, Separation, Divorce, and Your Rights**, $8.85
_____copies of **Real Estate Buying/Selling Guide for Washington**, $8.95
_____copies of **Keeping Track**, $14.95
_____copies of **Keeping Track Case**, $10.95
_____copies of **Keeping Track Pak**, $24.95
_____copies of **Financial Freedom on $5 a Day**, $10.95
Please add $3.00 for postage & handling.
WA residents, include 7.8% sales tax.